MW00529460

# Phoenix

## by Scott Organ

A SAMUEL FRENCH ACTING EDITION

SAMUEL FRENCH

FOUNDED 1830

NEW YORK HOLLYWOOD LONDON TORONTO

SAMUELFRENCH.COM

**ISBN 978-0-573-69885-9**          Printed in U.S.A.          #29656

## MUSIC USE NOTE

Licensees are solely responsible for obtaining formal written permission from copyright owners to use copyrighted music in the performance of this play and are strongly cautioned to do so. If no such permission is obtained by the licensee, then the licensee must use only original music that the licensee owns and controls. Licensees are solely responsible and liable for all music clearances and shall indemnify the copyright owners of the play and their licensing agent, Samuel French, Inc., against any costs, expenses, losses and liabilities arising from the use of music by licensees.

## IMPORTANT BILLING AND CREDIT REQUIREMENTS

All producers of *PHOENIX must* give credit to the Author of the Play in all programs distributed in connection with performances of the Play, and in all instances in which the title of the Play appears for the purposes of advertising, publicizing or otherwise exploiting the Play and/or a production. The name of the Author *must* appear on a separate line on which no other name appears, immediately following the title and *must* appear in size of type not less than fifty percent of the size of the title type.

In addition the following credit *must* be given in all programs and publicity information distributed in association with this piece:

**Phoenix premiered at the 34th Humana Festival of<br>
New American Plays at<br>
Actors Theatre of Louisville on March 5, 2010**

**Phoenix received its Off-Broadway premiere produced by<br>
The Barrow Group Theatre<br>
In the TGB Studio Theater on April 10, 2010**

*PHOENIX* had its world premiere at the 2010 Humana Festival of New American Plays at Actors Theatre of Louisville (Marc Masterson, artistic director), and was directed by Aaron Posner, with sets by Michael B. Raiford, costumes by Lorraine Venberg, lighting by Jeff Nellis, sound by Benjamin Marcum, props by Mark Walston, and dramaturgy by Sarah Lunnie. The production stage manager was Kimberley J. First. The cast was as follows:

**SUE** . . . . . . . . . . . . . . . . . . . . . . . . . . . . . . . . . . . . . . . . . . . . . . . . . Suli Holum
**BRUCE** . . . . . . . . . . . . . . . . . . . . . . . . . . . . . . . . . . . . . . . . . . . . . . Trey Lyford

## CHARACTERS

**SUE** – A woman in her 30s.
**BRUCE** – A man in his 30s.

## SETTING

New York, NY, and Phoenix, AZ

## TIME

The Present

## Scene One

*(**BRUCE** and **SUE**, in a coffee shop.)*

**SUE.** Three things.

**BRUCE.** Oh, okay.

**SUE.** Yeah.

**BRUCE.** We're diving right in.

**SUE.** There's three things I want to say.

**BRUCE.** Okay. Good things come in threes, right? Isn't that what they say?

**SUE.** Deaths.

**BRUCE.** Sorry?

**SUE.** And deaths. Come in threes. Is what they say. And good things too.

**BRUCE.** Okay. Well. Before you start, let me just be the first to say welcome back.

**SUE.** Thank you.

**BRUCE.** What did that mean "let me be the first to say?"

**SUE.** I don't know.

**BRUCE.** I'm the only one here.

**SUE.** No big deal.

**BRUCE.** How about this – welcome back.

**SUE.** Thanks again.

**BRUCE.** And how was it?

**SUE.** Uh, the trip? It was okay. It was business.

**BRUCE.** I wasn't sure I would hear from you.

**SUE.** You did. You are.

**BRUCE.** It's been a while. It's been…what? A month?

**SUE.** Four weeks.

**BRUCE.** A month, right?

7

**SUE.** No. Four weeks isn't really…

**BRUCE.** Okay, right. Four weeks.

**SUE.** I was away.

**BRUCE.** On business.

**SUE.** That's right.

**BRUCE.** Well. Welcome back.

**SUE.** Thank you.

**BRUCE.** A good trip?

**SUE.** I guess. Neither good nor bad.

**BRUCE.** Okay.

**SUE.** Yeah. No, it was fine.

**BRUCE.** All right. Number one.

**SUE.** What?

**BRUCE.** You had three things.

**SUE.** Oh. For a second I thought that was like a catch phrase or something…

**BRUCE.** Which?

**SUE.** You said "number one." Like "number one."

**BRUCE.** Meaning?

**SUE.** No. Let's just…

**BRUCE.** Right. The three. Let's hear it.

**SUE.** One.

**BRUCE.** *(pretending it's his catch phrase –)* Number One.

**SUE.** What?

**BRUCE.** No, it's a…Go ahead.

**SUE.** The first thing I wanted to tell you. Before I left town.

**BRUCE.** Back then, yes…*Four* weeks ago.

**SUE.** Is I had a great time with you that night.

**BRUCE.** Me too.

**SUE.** I did. On that…you know, it didn't even qualify as a date…

**BRUCE.** Drinks, or…

**SUE.** Yeah.

**BRUCE.** Me too. I thought we really hit it off.

**SUE.** Yeah.

**BRUCE.** And the whole, crazy night, it was funny, it felt like we were stupid college kids or something.

**SUE.** We actually were kind of stupid.

**BRUCE.** But, yes, it was fun, the whole…I was going to say date.

**SUE.** Hook up, I guess.

**BRUCE.** Better than that. Drinks.

**SUE.** Well.

**BRUCE.** Just the hanging out, you know? Talking, and…as a team, you know, our silver medal performance in the trivia thing.

**SUE.** We were robbed.

**BRUCE.** My fault…

**SUE.** No…

**BRUCE.** It was…

**SUE.** Absolutely not. To say no one is buried in Grant's Tomb…

**BRUCE.** Yeah…

**SUE.** That he's "entombed –"

**BRUCE.** "Entombed."

**SUE.** Not buried. Is…

**BRUCE.** I agree.

**SUE.** We were robbed.

**BRUCE.** You are so good at trivia. You are. You're very trivial…minded…You're smart.

**SUE.** Well, it was fun.

**BRUCE.** And, you know, I hadn't planned on things going where they did. You know, later.

**SUE.** I thought they might.

**BRUCE.** And…You did?

**SUE.** Yes.

**BRUCE.** Oh. Well. I wasn't going to presume, or hope that…I just didn't really have a plan, per se, in my head.

**SUE.** I knew.

**BRUCE.** You did?

**SUE.** I know myself. And I liked you.

**BRUCE.** Liked me?

**SUE.** That night. You know, and still. You're a great guy.

**BRUCE.** Thanks.

**SUE.** You're a little weird.

**BRUCE.** Oh.

**SUE.** Yeah. You are.

**BRUCE.** Okay.

**SUE.** But I think that's okay. There's good weird and there's bad weird.

**BRUCE.** Right. Bad, like, come look at my homemade chain mail armor that I made with my own two hands...

**SUE.** You have chain mail armor?

**BRUCE.** No, I'm saying if...

**SUE.** Yes. And no. There's worse weird, believe me.

**BRUCE.** Or I'm in a barbershop quartet.

**SUE.** Depends. I feel like some guys could pull that off.

**BRUCE.** I'm not in one.

**SUE.** Depending on who you are.

**BRUCE.** I'm not in one.

**SUE.** That's fine.

**BRUCE.** Do you think that I should look into it?

**SUE.** A barbershop quartet?

**BRUCE.** Yes.

**SUE.** No.

**BRUCE.** Then we are agreed. See, I knew we get along.

**SUE.** Yeah. No, it was fun. That night.

**BRUCE.** Agreed once again.

**SUE.** Better than most.

**BRUCE.** Okay, I can live with that. "Better than most." I won't put it on my headstone, but...

**SUE.** Meaning. Meeting strangers. Your odds, you know. They suck.

**BRUCE.** Right.

**SUE.** Not better than most.

**BRUCE.** Okay.

**SUE.** As far as drinks with strangers go, that was my most enjoyable yet.

**BRUCE.** Number One!

**SUE.** I get it.

**BRUCE.** Sorry.

**SUE.** No, it's kind of funny, actually.

**BRUCE.** Most enjoyable yet for me too.

**SUE.** Okay.

**BRUCE.** Just handing out the superlatives now, aren't we?

**SUE.** Yes.

**BRUCE.** Bestest not-quite-date ever.

**SUE.** Yeah, and –

**BRUCE.** I'm just glad you called, and I'm glad to see you in person and it had been a while and I was holding out hope, but it had been a bit, so I was a little nervous I wouldn't hear from you, but here you are.

**SUE.** Here I am.

**BRUCE.** Yes. Time had passed. A month. Or, you know, nearly –

**SUE.** Right.

**BRUCE.** Which was enough time for me to think, "Okay, I get the point…"

**SUE.** Yeah, well…

**BRUCE.** And think, "Next time, Bruce, get the girl's number, too," you know?

**SUE.** Sure.

**BRUCE.** Don't just settle with handing yours over. It's fundamental. But, damn, that was fun, right, that night?

**SUE.** Yeah, it was.

**BRUCE.** Right? And here you are. You called.

**SUE.** Yeah.

**BRUCE.** Awesome.

**SUE.** And I should get to the second thing.

**BRUCE.** Let's do this.

**SUE.** Okay, then.

**BRUCE.** I like your style. It's very, you know…

**SUE.** Okay.

**BRUCE.** Hit me.

**SUE.** Bearing in mind all that I said…

**BRUCE.** *(I'm)* Bearing…

**SUE.** I can't see you anymore.

> *(Pause. He begins waving in front of her face.)*

**BRUCE.** I'm right here. Right here.

> *(pause)*

I didn't expect that.

**SUE.** Are you bearing in mind still?

**BRUCE.** Is that supposed to take the sting out?

**SUE.** I guess it is.

**BRUCE.** What? That you like hanging out with me but you don't want to see me anymore so, what? It kind of evens out?

**SUE.** Yes?

> *(pause)*

**BRUCE.** There's somebody else?

**SUE.** No.

**BRUCE.** You sure?

**SUE.** Yes.

**BRUCE.** Because then I would understand.

**SUE.** Then yes. Someone else. My husband, in fact.

**BRUCE.** No one else.

**SUE.** No.

**BRUCE.** You just prefer the company of say, no one, over, say, me.

**SUE.** I like you. I just don't want to be involved with anyone right now.

**BRUCE.** I hear you.

**SUE.** Good.

**BRUCE.** I mean, I hear you. Dinner for one, nothing like it.

**SUE.** Right…

**BRUCE.** You know. A can of soup is just the right size for… And sprawling all across the bed. The great long late nights alone with not a fucking soul to talk to except your two cats…

**SUE.** You should probably get out more.

**BRUCE.** You know what, Sue? I probably should.

*(pause)*

**SUE.** How did you know I have two cats?

**BRUCE.** I didn't.

**SUE.** I do.

**BRUCE.** Congratulations.

**SUE.** Thank you.

**BRUCE.** Cats don't live forever, you know.

**SUE.** Yeah.

**BRUCE.** I'm sorry. That sounded mean.

**SUE.** It's just the truth.

**BRUCE.** Well. Just because it's the truth doesn't mean I have to spout it out all the time.

**SUE.** It's not a problem.

**BRUCE.** You know, "More than 25 million people have died of AIDS."

**SUE.** Really?

**BRUCE.** Just because it's true doesn't mean I have to spout it out.

**SUE.** Is anyone doing anything about AIDS, I mean, seriously…

**BRUCE.** Well. I won't lie to you…

**SUE.** Don't.

**BRUCE.** I am sorry you're not interested. I am.

**SUE.** It's not you. I just…it's not something I want to do right now. I was away and I was thinking about my life, about the world, and…

**BRUCE.** And what?

**SUE.** And I just thought…

**BRUCE.** What?

**SUE.** I don't know. I don't know.

**BRUCE.** You should figure that out.

**SUE.** Well, no, I don't really have to figure any fucking thing out.

**BRUCE.** Of course not. I'm sorry.

(*pause*)

Yeah. Sorry.

**SUE.** Forget it.

**BRUCE.** Our first and last fight.

**SUE.** Yeah.

**BRUCE.** Not bad. Only one fight.

**SUE.** Not bad.

**BRUCE.** You keep the cats.

**SUE.** Thanks.

**BRUCE.** We'll split up the books later.

**SUE.** Yeah.

(*pause*)

I should go. I need to go.

**BRUCE.** Okay.

**SUE.** I have to check in at work.

**BRUCE.** Okay.

**SUE.** Well, Bruce. It was nice to talk to you.

**BRUCE.** And you.

**SUE.** It was nice to see you and I wish you all the best.

*(pause)*

In all your future endeavors. Whatever they may be.

**BRUCE.** Right back at you.

*(She starts out.)*

Sue.

**SUE.** Yeah?

**BRUCE.** Three.

**SUE.** What?

**BRUCE.** Number three?

**SUE.** Oh.

**BRUCE.** Yeah.

**SUE.** Right. I said three.

**BRUCE.** You did.

**SUE.** Forget it.

**BRUCE.** No, no.

**SUE.** Uh…

**BRUCE.** Let's hear it.

**SUE.** Yeah…

**BRUCE.** So far it's – one, I like you. Two, let's never see each other again. I'm really looking forward to three. What could it be?

**SUE.** It's, uhh…

**BRUCE.** Come on. You said three.

**SUE.** Remember, of all the myriad things we discussed that night, and you said you couldn't have kids…

**BRUCE.** Yeah.

**SUE.** Yeah, well…

**BRUCE.** Great first date material. Genius.

**SUE.** Well – we were talking about everything.

**BRUCE.** Oh, fuck.

**SUE.** What?

**BRUCE.** That's why.

**SUE.** What?

**BRUCE.** You want children.

**SUE.** No.

**BRUCE.** Of course.

**SUE.** I told you I didn't. That's why it came up.

**BRUCE.** Of course you would say that now.

**SUE.** No, I said it first, I said I don't want kids and then you told me…

**BRUCE.** Stupid, stupid me.

**SUE.** No, that's not it. Seriously.

**BRUCE.** What then?

**SUE.** Well.

**BRUCE.** Go ahead.

**SUE.** You can.

**BRUCE.** I can what?

**SUE.** You can have kids.

**BRUCE.** Why?

**SUE.** I don't really know why.

**BRUCE.** Well, no. How do you know?

**SUE.** Because I'm pregnant.

**BRUCE.** Right, right, right.

**SUE.** Yeah.

*(pause)*

**BRUCE.** With whose?

**SUE.** Whose?

**BRUCE.** Uh-huh…

**SUE.** With you.

**BRUCE.** Me.

**SUE.** Yeah. That's what I'm trying to tell you.

**BRUCE.** With me.

**SUE.** Yes.

**BRUCE.** Me.

**SUE.** Yes.

**BRUCE.** But I can't.

**SUE.** You can. You can. I thought you should know.

*(pause)*

So, you know, now you know something new about yourself.

**BRUCE.** Okay. We were careful still.

**SUE.** Not careful enough.

**BRUCE.** Right.

**SUE.** I thought this was something you should know.

**BRUCE.** Right.

**SUE.** That you deserved to know.

**BRUCE.** And there's been no one else.

**SUE.** No one else.

**BRUCE.** Really?

**SUE.** I would remember. I remember those things. Sex. With people.

**BRUCE.** Wow. I was told I couldn't.

**SUE.** I know.

**BRUCE.** That's what they told me. That's what the doctors told me.

**SUE.** Well. They were wrong. And no worries – I am going to take care of it.

**BRUCE.** Take care of the baby?

**SUE.** Take care of the situation.

**BRUCE.** Oh. Oh.

**SUE.** Yes. I'll take care of it. I don't need any help is what I'm saying.

**BRUCE.** Oh.

**SUE.** Financial, or otherwise. No worries.

**BRUCE.** No worries.

**SUE.** Yeah.

**BRUCE.** Holy shit.

**SUE.** What?

**BRUCE.** Really?

**SUE.** Yeah. I thought you should know.

**BRUCE.** Yeah.

**SUE.** It seemed the right thing to do.

**BRUCE.** Thank you.

**SUE.** I have to go now.

**BRUCE.** What?

**SUE.** So. Once again. Thanks for a fun night.

**BRUCE.** Really?

**SUE.** What?

**BRUCE.** And now you're just walking out the door?

**SUE.** I have work. I have to check in with them.

**BRUCE.** I feel like you've chucked a grenade on me and now you're permanently walking out forever.

**SUE.** I have to check in with work. I just got back into town last night.

**BRUCE.** Isn't there more that we need to talk about?

**SUE.** I don't think so, no. It's pretty straightforward.

**BRUCE.** Is it?

**SUE.** Yeah. For me, at least.

**BRUCE.** But we're, you know, even if it's…some weird…. I mean, this is something we've shared, or…you've dropped this grenade on my lap. Because I was told that I couldn't.

**SUE.** Yes. They were wrong. And I really do apologize but I have to leave.

**BRUCE.** I feel –

**SUE.** I'm sorry.

**BRUCE.** I feel the least you could do is talk to me…

**SUE.** I can't.

**BRUCE.** For a few moments at least.

**SUE.** I can't.

**BRUCE.** A few minutes out of your entire life you could loan some out to me to let me register this, to talk about this with you, for whom without this would never be happening. Can you not give me that?

**SUE.** No.

**BRUCE.** Not even that? Not even that?

**SUE.** No.

*(He looks shocked. Pause.)*

At least not now. Not now. Later maybe I can find a little time.

**BRUCE.** That would be nice.

**SUE.** We'll see.

**BRUCE.** Beyond nice, it would be a tremendous act of charity...

**SUE.** Can I call you later?

**BRUCE.** Will you?

**SUE.** I'll try.

**BRUCE.** If you try you will succeed.

**SUE.** Yeah.

**BRUCE.** Calling is easy. I can show you.

**SUE.** No.

**BRUCE.** I can even set you up so you press just one single number and it will call me.

**SUE.** Okay...

**BRUCE.** It's called speed dial.

**SUE.** I'll call you.

**BRUCE.** Okay, then.

*(He sticks out his hand.)*

**SUE.** What is that?

**BRUCE.** A handshake. A deal.

*(She hesitates.)*

I know it's one huge hell of a commitment thing, this having to place a phone call to me, but...

*(She shakes his hand. Lights out.)*

## Scene Two

*(A phone ringing.* **BRUCE** *and* **SUE** *on their phones, apart.)*

**BRUCE.** *(looking first at his phone –)* If it isn't my old friend "restricted caller."

**SUE.** Keeps the stalkers at bay.

**BRUCE.** Am I a stalker?

**SUE.** You have potential…

**BRUCE.** Someone who finally believes in me.

**SUE.** But to the point.

**BRUCE.** Right. Okay.

**SUE.** I don't have a lot of time…

**BRUCE.** Okay. My turn for three things.

**SUE.** Okay.

**BRUCE.** Maybe three. Depending on what you say.

**SUE.** Okay.

**BRUCE.** Seriously. Thank you for taking the time to call.

**SUE.** No problem.

**BRUCE.** I really appreciate it…

**SUE.** It's fine. Let's just go ahead.

**BRUCE.** Oh. Okay.

**SUE.** Yeah.

**BRUCE.** One is – have you…

**SUE.** Have I?

**BRUCE.** You know…

**SUE.** No, I don't.

**BRUCE.** What is it they say – terminated…the pregnancy?

**SUE.** Abortion is another term you may have heard.

**BRUCE.** Yeah.

**SUE.** Have I done that yet?

**BRUCE.** Yes.

**SUE.** No, I have not.

**BRUCE.** Oh.

**SUE.** Not yet.

**BRUCE.** Okay. Then two: When are you doing that?

**SUE.** Why?

**BRUCE.** I just wanted to know.

**SUE.** In a week or so.

**BRUCE.** Oh.

**SUE.** Yeah.

**BRUCE.** You have to wait? I mean, I don't even know...

**SUE.** It's a scheduling thing.

**BRUCE.** Oh.

**SUE.** I'm going to a facility – a place I'm very familiar with.

**BRUCE.** Okay.

**SUE.** It's a clinic that I know and trust.

**BRUCE.** You're a nurse.

**SUE.** That's right.

**BRUCE.** So you know people.

**SUE.** I do.

**BRUCE.** You're a...what are you...you're a traveling nurse?

**SUE.** That's right.

**BRUCE.** And what is that?

**SUE.** Well. It's a nurse. Who travels.

   *(pause)*

**BRUCE.** Have I done something to piss you off?

**SUE.** You've impregnated me.

**BRUCE.** I didn't mean to.

**SUE.** I know.

**BRUCE.** Not only did I not mean to, I didn't think it was physically possible.

**SUE.** I know.

**BRUCE.** You were, as I recall, rather forthright in the removal of my pants.

**SUE.** On a side-note, you should, you know, consider rotating your stock...

**BRUCE.** What?

**SUE.** Your so-called "protection."

**BRUCE.** If you're implying that my condoms were somehow old as a result of a lack of sexual activity on my part in recent, what, years, then, you know, you're dead on.

**SUE.** I'm just saying, they have expiration dates.

**BRUCE.** Mine don't.

**SUE.** Because, I think, yours pre-date the modern practice of listing the expiration date.

**BRUCE.** Oh, man.

**SUE.** Look. It's just this whole thing is a bit of a pain in the ass, and I agreed to call and talk, briefly, with you, and you're not necessarily making anything easier with the…casual conversation…the "tell me about your job" blah blah blah…

(*BRUCE looks a little like he's been punched. A pause.*)

I signed up with an agency. I travel to different hospitals and facilities all over the country, sometimes outside the country, and I work for short periods of time, usually three months or so, and then I go somewhere else.

**BRUCE.** All the time.

**SUE.** Pretty much.

**BRUCE.** But you live here.

**SUE.** No. Not really.

**BRUCE.** Really?

**SUE.** Yeah.

**BRUCE.** You don't live here?

**SUE.** No.

**BRUCE.** This never came up that night.

**SUE.** I find it takes away from a first date, telling the other person you don't actually live here.

**BRUCE.** Wow.

**SUE.** My mother lives here. I come here a few times a year.

**BRUCE.** You didn't tell me this.

**SUE.** You know what, Bruce? Had I – we wouldn't have had such a good time.

**BRUCE.** And we wouldn't be pregnant.

**SUE.** *We* aren't pregnant.

**BRUCE.** Okay.

**SUE.** I'm sorry I didn't mention it that night.

**BRUCE.** So when you said you were going away on business, you weren't just going away on business?

**SUE.** No.

**BRUCE.** You were leaving for…what?

**SUE.** Three months.

**BRUCE.** So when you said you would call me when you got back?

**SUE.** I misrepresented when I would be getting back.

**BRUCE.** Misrepresented.

**SUE.** I lied.

**BRUCE.** So you did. And why are you back?

**SUE.** Nothing. Just coincidence. Job stuff.

**BRUCE.** Oh.

**SUE.** My job ran short and I'm being reassigned.

**BRUCE.** So I just got lucky then.

**SUE.** Depending on how you look at it.

**BRUCE.** That you happened to be back in town and happened to call.

**SUE.** I never would have even told you if you hadn't told me that you couldn't have kids.

**BRUCE.** I never would've heard from you.

**SUE.** Probably not.

**BRUCE.** No.

**SUE.** No. Definitely not.

**BRUCE.** Okay.

**SUE.** I don't want to be in a relationship.

**BRUCE.** I've gathered.

**SUE.** Yeah.

**BRUCE.** At least not with me.

**SUE.** No, that's not true. I liked you.

**BRUCE.** There you go again with the past tense…

**SUE.** Because, Bruce, and I am truly sorry if this sounds harsh, but you are past tense.

**BRUCE.** I already am.

**SUE.** I thought I made that clear. But you made me shake your hand. And here we are.

(*pause*)

So what's number three?

(*He says nothing.*)

I've upset you.

**BRUCE.** No.

**SUE.** I've called you past tense.

**BRUCE.** You did do that.

(*a beat*)

**SUE.** Look. If I am short with you, it's because I have a whole army of brutal hormones fucking in a huge way with my body right now.

**BRUCE.** You do?

**SUE.** You know what? I knew we had conceived. I knew it when it happened.

**BRUCE.** How could you know something like that?

**SUE.** I felt it.

**BRUCE.** Really?

**SUE.** I know that seems crazy but it's true. And I ignored it because I thought we had been safe and remembered you telling me that you couldn't have kids. But I gotta tell you – the hormones kicked in right away. They're quite the tremendous force, let me tell you.

**BRUCE.** Thanks for telling me that.

**SUE.** I don't know what the fuck is going on, really. I don't recognize myself. I want to kill most people. I want to sleep. I want to eat all the time except when I want to throw up.

**BRUCE.** Sorry…

**SUE.** Would you like to know what I had for lunch?

**BRUCE.** Of course.

**SUE.** Two big disgusting bearclaws. For lunch.

**BRUCE.** Yum.

**SUE.** I'm a healthy eater.

**BRUCE.** I like a bearclaw.

**SUE.** Don't say that word.

**BRUCE.** Bearclaw?

**SUE.** Stop.

**BRUCE.** Sorry. You said it.

**SUE.** Do you want me to vomit?

**BRUCE.** No, I don't.

**SUE.** You see? This is what I've been reduced to. And to top it all off, I have another week of this.

**BRUCE.** I'm sorry.

**SUE.** It's not your fault.

**BRUCE.** Nonetheless.

**SUE.** Or it is your fault.

**BRUCE.** I am so sick of you bad-mouthing my condoms.

*(She smiles at this.)*

I didn't know you'd feel the pregnancy so soon.

**SUE.** You do. At least I do. Pretty damn soon. It's just a pain in the ass. And I am eager to have it done with. So if I seem to be…

**BRUCE.** No. It's okay.

**SUE.** You want to tell me your third thing?

**BRUCE.** Uh…

**SUE.** No, go ahead. The hormones have spiked or something. I won't snap at you. I promise.

**BRUCE.** You sure?

**SUE.** I promise.

**BRUCE.** Okay. The third thing – may I come with you.

**SUE.** Come with me where?

**BRUCE.** When you…terminate the pregnancy.

**SUE.** May you come with me?

**BRUCE.** Yes.

**SUE.** No.

**BRUCE.** No?

**SUE.** No. What the hell kind of question is that?

**BRUCE.** A stupid one, I guess.

**SUE.** Yes.

**BRUCE.** A stupid one.

   *(pause)*

**SUE.** Why? Why would you want to do that?

**BRUCE.** Because. I'm not exactly sure. Because I'm in-volved…

**SUE.** Nominally.

**BRUCE.** Biologically.

   *(pause)*

   Look. I'm not trying to insert my will into all of this. I realize that's not my place.

**SUE.** That's good.

**BRUCE.** And frankly it's not as if I want you to do anything different than what you want to.

**SUE.** Good. Because you would get nowhere with that.

**BRUCE.** No. I don't…. I don't want kids. I really don't.

**SUE.** Okay.

**BRUCE.** I just want to be party to this thing that has hap-pened…

**SUE.** Nothing has really happened.

**BRUCE.** No?

**SUE.** No. Nothing of consequence.

**BRUCE.** To you, perhaps.

**SUE.** Yes, to me.

**BRUCE.** I didn't even know that I could have kids.

**SUE.** And now you know. But that is unrelated to this. It's of no consequence.

**BRUCE.** I want to come along.

**SUE.** Why?

**BRUCE.** I can't explain it. All I know is I feel very compelled to be there. To…participate in it. To…live it.

**SUE.** You realize your "participation" would be sitting on a shitty couch reading an old copy of Rolling Stone?

**BRUCE.** That's fine.

**SUE.** It's a procedure. A relatively simple one at that. It's fucking outpatient.

**BRUCE.** I understand that.

**SUE.** And you still want to be there?

**BRUCE.** I do.

**SUE.** Well, no.

**BRUCE.** I insist.

**SUE.** You can't insist. You have no right to insist.

**BRUCE.** Okay, it seems you got me there.

**SUE.** Yeah, well…

**BRUCE.** Look. I just want to be there. I do. And though I may have no rights, per se, I ask you to let me do this. That, and then I leave you alone. I'll just meet you there – I'll read the Rolling Stone – you'll come out, we'll say hi, and then that's that.

**SUE.** That's that?

**BRUCE.** Yeah.

**SUE.** Why?

**BRUCE.** I don't exactly know. I don't.

**SUE.** You supply your own transportation?

**BRUCE.** Of course.

**SUE.** And afterwards, that's that?

**BRUCE.** My word.

**SUE.** Okay, then.

**BRUCE.** Really?

**SUE.** Yes. You want to meet me there, I won't stop you.

**BRUCE.** So that's a yes?

**SUE.** That is a yes.

**BRUCE.** Thank you.

**SUE.** No problem.

**BRUCE.** So when are you doing it?

**SUE.** Next Wednesday.

**BRUCE.** Okay, great. Where?

**SUE.** Phoenix.

**BRUCE.** Phoenix…? Is that the name of the facility?

**SUE.** That's the name of the city.

**BRUCE.** What city?

**SUE.** The city where the clinic is.

**BRUCE.** Phoenix, Arizona?

**SUE.** Yes.

**BRUCE.** Phoenix, Phoenix?

**SUE.** Yes. My next job. Phoenix.

**BRUCE.** Next Wednesday way the hell off in Phoenix. Arizona.

**SUE.** That's right.

(long pause)

**BRUCE.** What time?

**SUE.** What?

**BRUCE.** What time is your appointment?

**SUE.** Oh, come on.

**BRUCE.** Come on what?

**SUE.** You're not coming to Phoenix.

**BRUCE.** Yes, I am.

**SUE.** Bruce…

**BRUCE.** I think so, yes. So, you know, where do I go? And what time?

**SUE.** I don't know. I haven't worked out all the details.

**BRUCE.** Okay. Well. Will you call me when you do?

(beat)

You said yes.

**SUE.** Fine. I'll call you the night before.

**BRUCE.** That's the best you can do?

**SUE.** Do you want me to call?

**BRUCE.** Fine. Will you shake on that? Metaphorically speaking?

**SUE.** What's with you and shaking?

**BRUCE.** It used to mean something. It means something to me.

**SUE.** Okay, fine.

(**BRUCE** *does a shaking motion.*)

**BRUCE.** Are you shaking?

(*She isn't.*)

**SUE.** Yes.

**BRUCE.** You promise?

**SUE.** Yes.

(*They shake.*)

**BRUCE.** Okay. See you Wednesday.

**SUE.** Right. Okay.

(*Lights out.*)

## Scene Three

*(BRUCE has two coffees – he holds one out to SUE.)*

**BRUCE.** Cream, right?

**SUE.** Bruce.

**BRUCE.** No cream? I was sure it was cream. They were about to close so I had to make some executive decisions. Decaf, because of the hour, I hope that's okay.

**SUE.** Bruce.

**BRUCE.** They're closed. I thought we could walk or something.

**SUE.** What are you doing here? When I called you I fully expected to catch you at home...

**BRUCE.** I told you I would come.

**SUE.** I thought you might have a modicum of what some people call "common sense."

**BRUCE.** And thanks for meeting up with me tonight. I know we didn't phone-shake on that part.

**SUE.** You drove for like three days all the way out here. What was I supposed to do?

**BRUCE.** I wasn't expecting anything.

**SUE.** That's good.

**BRUCE.** I told you that. My arm is starting to hurt.

*(She takes the coffee.)*

**SUE.** Bruce. It's certifiable. Really. Think about it. And yes, I take cream.

**BRUCE.** I have a backlog of vacation. Use it or lose it, you know? And I've always wanted to go to the Grand Canyon State.

**SUE.** They have flights, you know. They actually fly planes out here.

**BRUCE.** You haven't been?

**SUE.** Where? What are you talking about?

**BRUCE.** The Grand Canyon.

**SUE.** No.

BRUCE. It's, uh…worth seeing.

SUE. Okay.

BRUCE. That's a big understatement.

You're here for three months, right?

SUE. Roughly, yes.

BRUCE. You should go.

SUE. I probably should.

BRUCE. Definitely. Definitely.

SUE. You're insane.

BRUCE. It's like a four hour drive from here. It's nothing. I'm telling you – It's, uhh…you can't perceive the depth of the thing. Or I couldn't. Because I have nothing to compare it to. I've never seen anything that deep, you know? It's uhh, really moving. Makes you really think.

SUE. About what?

BRUCE. I don't know. Time, you know. Time. The great tremendous past.

SUE. Yeah, well. I have a hard enough time with the present.

BRUCE. It makes you feel pretty insignificant.

SUE. Why would you intentionally choose to feel insignificant?

BRUCE. It's liberating in a way, don't you think?

SUE. No. I don't. Sounds like it sucks.

BRUCE. You know what?

SUE. What?

BRUCE. You seemed more fun on our date.

SUE. I am fun. I am.

BRUCE. Okay.

SUE. I am so much fun. That's a ridiculous thing to say about me.

BRUCE. Sorry.

SUE. You should see how much fun I am.

BRUCE. Okay.

**SUE.** Okay, what?

**BRUCE.** Let's see it.

**SUE.** It's not like I...I don't just do fun on command.

**BRUCE.** Okay.

**SUE.** I was fun on that date.

**BRUCE.** You were.

**SUE.** Right?

**BRUCE.** So much fun, we're in Phoenix.

**SUE.** Yeah, well.

**BRUCE.** No. That night was a lot of fun for me.

**SUE.** Okay, then. See?

**BRUCE.** Yes. I stand corrected. You're fun.

   *(pause)*

**SUE.** So. The Grand Canyon.

**BRUCE.** Yeah.

**SUE.** It's...what? How old? It's...what? The earth is billions of years old...?

**BRUCE.** 6,000.

**SUE.** What?

**BRUCE.** The earth is 6,000 years old. Roughly.

**SUE.** Uh.

**BRUCE.** Grand Canyon was created by the flood.

**SUE.** The flood.

**BRUCE.** Yeah.

**SUE.** The one with Noah.

**BRUCE.** Yep.

   *(pause)*

**SUE.** *(to no one in particular –)* Check.

**BRUCE.** It's a joke.

**SUE.** Oh. Well. I don't really know you, so...

**BRUCE.** It's a joke.

**SUE.** Okay.

**BRUCE.** I think the earth is 4 or 5 billion years old.

**SUE.** I thought I was old.

**BRUCE.** No. You're not old.

**SUE.** 4 or 5 billion?

**BRUCE.** I think so.

(**SUE** *ponders this.*)

**SUE.** Okay, then. But. Did you know?

**BRUCE.** What?

**SUE.** I read this thing – there are these scientists who say that the science is there or will be there to time travel.

**BRUCE.** Sounds good.

**SUE.** You'd think, yes. You'd think. But here's the thing.

**BRUCE.** What?

**SUE.** If that's true, which some very reputable people say is true, then where are the time travel tourists?

**BRUCE.** What are they?

**SUE.** Where are the people from the future who come back here?

**BRUCE.** Not here yet.

**SUE.** Why not?

**BRUCE.** I don't know.

**SUE.** Well, I do.

**BRUCE.** Tell me.

**SUE.** Because they aren't coming back. They haven't which means they won't. Because if they had we would know. Which could only mean one thing.

**BRUCE.** What?

**SUE.** It could only mean that this world, at least as we know it, will not be around for that much longer.

**BRUCE.** Really?

**SUE.** Yes. It's the only conclusion. In fact, there was a heavily-advertised time travelers convention – it was at MIT on May 7, 2005, designed for time travelers to all come back on that date…

**BRUCE.** No one showed.

**SUE.** A lot of people showed.

**BRUCE.** Oh. Really?

**SUE.** But none were from the future.

**BRUCE.** They didn't come back because the world as we know it isn't even going to be around for that much longer.

**SUE.** That's right.

**BRUCE.** Wow.

**SUE.** Yeah.

**BRUCE.** If that's true.

**SUE.** I think it is.

**BRUCE.** Then that sucks.

**SUE.** I thought you like feeling insignificant.

**BRUCE.** Not that insignificant.

**SUE.** I think it's about time, don't you?

**BRUCE.** For what?

**SUE.** Earth is old. Time to move on. Let 'er blow up.

**BRUCE.** You really believe that?

**SUE.** I do. Did you read what happened today?

**BRUCE.** No. What happened?

**SUE.** It doesn't even matter, really. Same old shit. Pick a day, read the paper. Doesn't matter.

**BRUCE.** What happened today?

**SUE.** Doesn't matter. It's just all very clear that we don't really learn a thing and we just play out the same shit over and over, over the millennia, and frankly, the sooner we fuck the planet, the better for the bacteria that are itching to take over.

**BRUCE.** Wow.

**SUE.** And you say I'm not fun.

**BRUCE.** I can't believe I'm about to do this...

**SUE.** What?

**BRUCE.** I shouldn't be bringing this up.

**SUE.** What?

**BRUCE.** But I feel given the depths of your morbidity, I
have no choice.

**SUE.** What?

**BRUCE.** And I am breaking all sorts of rules here…

**SUE.** Just tell me.

**BRUCE.** I'm that guy.

**SUE.** What guy?

**BRUCE.** The guy…from the future.

**SUE.** You're that guy?

**BRUCE.** I am that guy. Hi there.

**SUE.** Well. Wow. Welcome to the past.

**BRUCE.** Thank you.

**SUE.** I'm honored. You've come out to me.

**BRUCE.** You gave me no choice.

**SUE.** So what's the future like?

**BRUCE.** It's a lot like Battlestar Galactica. The original one.

**SUE.** Nice.

**BRUCE.** Yeah. It's not bad.

**SUE.** I'm glad to hear it.

**BRUCE.** Did you ever consider that maybe people from the
future don't tell the people in the past who they are?

**SUE.** Why wouldn't they? I would.

**BRUCE.** I'll tell you why – people can't handle it. People
can't handle very much in the way of outright truth.

**SUE.** I agree with you there.

**BRUCE.** If I went public, I'd end up in some subterranean
holding cell in Quantico, Virginia.

**SUE.** Possibly.

**BRUCE.** So we do it on the down low…We just come in
periodically to poke around, see what's going on.

**SUE.** Is that right? So why now?

**BRUCE.** Well. The truth?

**SUE.** Yeah.

**BRUCE.** Women from this era have a reputation for being kind of easy.

**SUE.** Oh yeah?

**BRUCE.** So guys come back looking for a little action.

**SUE.** A sex vacation in the past.

**BRUCE.** That's right. I hate to reduce it to this, but you're pretty much fish in a barrel.

**SUE.** Is that right?

**BRUCE.** In the future, men learn a great deal more about seduction which make us so efficient in this era.

**SUE.** You didn't seduce me.

**BRUCE.** That's how good I am.

**SUE.** Yeah, right.

**BRUCE.** If you see it, it ain't seduction.

**SUE.** Is that right?

**BRUCE.** It's a saying we have in the future.

**SUE.** So what other advancements do we have to look forward to?

**BRUCE.** Better batteries. Like, way better batteries that last hundreds of times longer.

**SUE.** That's positive.

**BRUCE.** Yeah, you won't believe the batteries of the future.

**SUE.** What else?

**BRUCE.** Turns out the Mormons were right.

**SUE.** Really?

**BRUCE.** Yeah. It was a big surprise to everyone. Except the Mormons. Latter Day all the way. It's another saying we have in the future.

**SUE.** Wow.

**BRUCE.** I'm kidding.

**SUE.** About being from the future?

**BRUCE.** About the Mormons. No, so far no God has made him, her or itself known. The big stuff is still mostly orchestrated by mankind. Things got really warm for a while. The size of the population became a lot more reasonable. Then the cold comes. Comes and stays.

SUE. What happened?

BRUCE. A massive meteor, smashing into the earth. Knocked off our axis. The electromagnetic field permanently altered. Nothing worked anymore. Nothing. Just a planet of very cold people, wandering around in the dark looking for food. As you can imagine, things got ugly.

SUE. Were you around for this?

BRUCE. This was way before me. After some very brutal thousands of years…

SUE. Still no God?

BRUCE. No God. Nowhere.

SUE. And you're telling me this why? To cheer me up?

BRUCE. I'm not done. People started to organize again. They did. It took a long time of warring and slavery and general brutality, but our better instincts came to fore.

SUE. See, I don't believe you.

BRUCE. No?

SUE. Our better instincts are merely a by-product of living a lucky life.

BRUCE. You think?

SUE. I do. We are all a hair away from being the savages we are at our core.

BRUCE. History proves you wrong. Future history. They started over. From scratch, they started over. The good guys organized and made it happen. And they had absolutely everything to relearn. Everything. It had all been forgotten. And they didn't do too bad. So you can stop stressing that it's all going to end.

SUE. Thanks. That's a load off.

BRUCE. Right? There is a reason to stick around.

SUE. I guess I have to take your word for it, being that I am merely from the present.

BRUCE. You do.

SUE. Okay. There's no Grand Canyon in the future?

**BRUCE.** I'm sad to say that there is not.

**SUE.** What happened to it?

**BRUCE.** It filled with sediment.

**SUE.** So you came all the way back here to see the Grand Canyon?

**BRUCE.** No.

**SUE.** Then what for?

**BRUCE.** To see you.

**SUE.** To see me.

**BRUCE.** Yeah.

**SUE.** Why me?

**BRUCE.** You seemed nice. At least on paper.

(*pause*)

**SUE.** Maybe you are bad weird.

**BRUCE.** Oh – I joined a barbershop quartet. I would sing for you but it kind defeats the purpose without my guys here.

**SUE.** No worries.

(*pause*)

**BRUCE.** It's getting late.

**SUE.** Yeah.

**BRUCE.** We have to get up early.

**SUE.** Yeah. Where are you staying?

**BRUCE.** The Taurus.

**SUE.** Is that a hotel?

**BRUCE.** My car.

**SUE.** Oh. You don't have a room?

**BRUCE.** No.

**SUE.** Oh. How come?

**BRUCE.** I don't know. There's some sort of convention in town.

**SUE.** Time Travelers?

**BRUCE.** Yep. I really have no excuse for not having gone further back into the past to book my room....

**SUE.** Stay at my place.

**BRUCE.** No, look, I told you I wouldn't bother you any more than briefly tomorrow.

**SUE.** Wait. You're actually going to say no to the Long Term Slash Short Term Inn & Lodge.

**BRUCE.** It does sound rather enchanting.

**SUE.** Right? They have a continental breakfast.

**BRUCE.** Hmm…Maybe if it were inter-continental.

**SUE.** Oh. It is. Muffins from the English.

**BRUCE.** Oh. Well. Toast from the French?

**SUE.** Absolutement.

**BRUCE.** Wow.

**SUE.** So…is that a oui?

**BRUCE.** For the Long Term Slash…

**SUE.** Short Term Inn & Lodge.

**BRUCE.** Inns I can do without. Hard to say no to a lodge though.

**SUE.** You are preaching to the choir.

**BRUCE.** Do they have hot chocolate?

**SUE.** No.

**BRUCE.** Okay, it's a deal.

**SUE.** Just don't try any of that sophisticated future seduction.

**BRUCE.** You got it.

**SUE.** Okay. You have to use your powers with a certain amount of responsibility.

**BRUCE.** Of course.

*(Lights out.)*

## Scene Four

*(**SUE**'s housing. They are half dressed. No one is saying anything.)*

**BRUCE.** It's just second nature, the whole seduction thing…

**SUE.** Of course.

**BRUCE.** Yeah. I can't really help it.

**SUE.** Right. At least we know I didn't get pregnant.

**BRUCE.** True.

**SUE.** I hope you understand that this is merely because I am lonely and in a new city.

**BRUCE.** Got it. Lonely. New city.

**SUE.** Or alone, rather. Which I don't mind.

**BRUCE.** Okay.

**SUE.** I'm alone. A little lonely. It breaks up the day.

**BRUCE.** Of course.

**SUE.** And nothing more.

**BRUCE.** It's okay – I'm on a sex vacation.

**SUE.** I forgot. Happy sex vacation.

**BRUCE.** Thank you. And thank you for participating.

**SUE.** Always eager to help a tourist.

**BRUCE.** So. Where are the cats?

**SUE.** With my mother. They're mine. But they live with my mother.

**BRUCE.** Can't even commit to the cats.

**SUE.** No.

**BRUCE.** Thanks for letting me stay.

**SUE.** It's no problem.

**BRUCE.** And you were right.

**SUE.** About what?

**BRUCE.** You are fun.

**SUE.** See?

**BRUCE.** You are.

**SUE.** I tried to tell you.

**BRUCE.** When you're not forecasting doom, you're okay.

**SUE.** Thanks.

**BRUCE.** You know. You and I, we're two for two.

**SUE.** How do you mean?

**BRUCE.** I mean, we've hung out a couple of times, and it's been fun.

**SUE.** Yeah. Tomorrow might put a dent in our numbers.

**BRUCE.** Doesn't it....

*(But he trails off.)*

**SUE.** Doesn't it what?

**BRUCE.** I don't know. We have a good time, you and I. Doesn't it seem to be a shame that we won't ever see each other again?

*(a beat)*

**SUE.** Let me ask you something.

**BRUCE.** Sure.

**SUE.** Are you just interested in me because I am being such a pain in the ass?

**BRUCE.** You mean, because you're playing hard to get?

**SUE.** You see, I'm not playing really.

**BRUCE.** You're just plain ole hard to get.

**SUE.** I suppose.

**BRUCE.** Well. That's a good question. Um. Probably partly.

**SUE.** You see?

**BRUCE.** But I think I would probably like you even if you weren't a pain in the ass, as much I enjoy pains in the ass.

**SUE.** My point is, here we are in Phoenix, Arizona, and I have been explicit with you that I am not interested in any sort of a relationship. And I keep putting you off and...

**BRUCE.** Was all this tonight putting me off?

**SUE.** Beyond that. I have not encouraged you and, being human, you find that attractive, or a challenge.

**BRUCE.** Perhaps I do.

**SUE.** But I'm just trying to remind you – take the game out of it and it's just people. And people, meaning me, are boring and petty and selfish, and if I were to sit here now with you and suddenly start twinkling about the eyes and asking you your favorite poem and movie and recipe and hanging on to your words as if they were the cure to cancer, then you would feel amused and emboldened for a while, until it became clear to you that there is no game in it at which point you would marshal your forces on the next nice ass that walks by.

**BRUCE.** Wow. You are…

**SUE.** What?

**BRUCE.** What is it you hope to get out of life? Really. Because I'm having a hard time imagining what it could be.

**SUE.** As few problems as possible. I want things to go smoothly. I don't want disappointment. I don't want to get my hopes up.

**BRUCE.** It's not all disappointment, you know.

**SUE.** It is. It is. It ultimately always is. You see, you say that to me, and fact is, that's bullshit, because you're gonna die. And how is your endgame anything other than a disappointment? To the people who love you? And in the interim, everyone is a terrified asshole, who given a few minor adjustments to their life, would so easily cut your fucking head off with a machete…

**BRUCE.** You think that?

**SUE.** Of course I think that. Of course. Our baser nature is our base nature. What in the hell have we learned? Really. Tell me.

**BRUCE.** And this is how your interest in nursing began?

**SUE.** No.

**BRUCE.** I was wondering.

**SUE.** It began when I was young and I needed a job to get me out of the house fast and they were hiring and paying for schooling and otherwise I may not have even made it this far. Don't get me wrong. My job requires compassion and that is something I actually have, believe it or not. In fact, I have so much compassion, I'm trying to save both of us from having to go through the annoyance and potential pain of an inevitably doomed relationship.

**BRUCE.** I don't need you to look out for me.

**SUE.** I think you do. I think you don't know any better. That's what I think.

**BRUCE.** Tell me why it's doomed.

**SUE.** It's doomed because I doom it. That's why. I don't even live anywhere. I don't. That's how I actually like it. And that's just one of many many reasons why I preemptively doom our relationship.

**BRUCE.** Let me just say this, I don't need you making decisions for me, out of whatever it is you think you have over me, your omniscience or whatever the hell you think it is you own.

**SUE.** I'm trying to save you some time and effort.

**BRUCE.** And furthermore. I'm not looking to get married to you. As you may recall, all I really said was that I thought it was a shame that we won't see each other again. And though it is obvious that I have some interest in you…

**SUE.** You drove to Phoenix to join me for my abortion.

**BRUCE.** Which is actually not really about you.

**SUE.** Fine.

**BRUCE.** And all I was saying was that it would be a shame. And I get you, I really do, and I get that you are trying to put me off, and I will confess to you that I may not be as incorrigible as you think, and that you are starting to have some success…

**SUE.** What do you mean?

**BRUCE.** That you are beginning to succeed in putting me off. You are winning that battle.

**SUE.** Okay, then.

**BRUCE.** It's working.

**SUE.** Okay.

**BRUCE.** I feel that I am beginning to like you less.

**SUE.** Great.

**BRUCE.** So – well done.

**SUE.** Thank you.

> *(Pause. She begins to re-dress.)*

**BRUCE.** Yes. Let's do that.

> *(He puts on his other clothes – they do this in silence. They finish. Long pause.)*

**SUE.** I'm sorry.

**BRUCE.** For what?

**SUE.** I'm just…sorry.

**BRUCE.** Okay.

**SUE.** Fact is.

**BRUCE.** What?

**SUE.** Fact is – I don't entirely dislike you.

**BRUCE.** I'm turning red from your effusions.

**SUE.** Will you let me talk in the way I would like to talk?

**BRUCE.** Okay.

**SUE.** I wouldn't be this stand-offish if it weren't for the fact that I like you too.

**BRUCE.** So this is what it feels like to be liked by you?

> *(a beat)*

All I was saying was – maybe next time you come see your mom or something, we could have a beer or something. Go bowling. That's really all I was saying.

> *(a beat)*

**SUE.** I like bowling.

**BRUCE.** I do too.

**SUE.** Me too.

**BRUCE.** That's all I'm saying. I just didn't want to drive out of here tomorrow without saying that maybe there could be a way to see each other again.

**SUE.** Okay.

**BRUCE.** And not will you marry me now.

**SUE.** Okay.

(*beat*)

Are you going to make me shake on something?

**BRUCE.** No.

**SUE.** Okay. Good.

**BRUCE.** I'm saying the equivalent of "call me next time you are in town and perhaps we could go bowling."

**SUE.** Okay. That's fine.

**BRUCE.** Okay then.

**SUE.** I'm not a very good bowler.

**BRUCE.** Well. You don't have to be.

**SUE.** Are you?

**BRUCE.** Not particularly.

**SUE.** Good.

**BRUCE.** I get lucky sometimes.

**SUE.** I don't.

**BRUCE.** And that's the crux of it.

**SUE.** The crux of what?

**BRUCE.** Bowling. Sometimes you get lucky, sometimes you don't.

**SUE.** I guess so. Why are we still up? We have to get up early.

**BRUCE.** It's already early. Look outside.

(*She does.*)

**SUE.** What should we do? We'd sleep for what – an hour?

**BRUCE.** I can't do that.

**SUE.** Me neither. Maybe we should just clean up and go out and get some coffee or something.

**BRUCE.** Catch the sunrise.

**SUE.** Yeah, okay.

**BRUCE.** Okay.

> *(pause)*

> Now?

**SUE.** Not just yet, no.

**BRUCE.** What are you doing?

**SUE.** Nothing.

**BRUCE.** Okay.

> *(They both are still for a moment. Lights out.)*

## Scene Five

*(The clinic.* SUE *and* BRUCE.*)*

**BRUCE.** Damn.

**SUE.** What?

**BRUCE.** You promised.

**SUE.** I promised what?

**BRUCE.** No Rolling Stone anywhere.

**SUE.** Oh, sorry.

**BRUCE.** I'll survive. How are you feeling?

**SUE.** Tired.

**BRUCE.** Me too. Nice place. Empty.

**SUE.** I know the nurses. The clinic doesn't actually open for an hour.

**BRUCE.** Aren't you fancy?

**SUE.** I am fancy. So is this worth the three-day drive?

**BRUCE.** I think so, yeah.

*(pause)*

In the future, having a child, you know, is so much easier.

**SUE.** Why is that?

**BRUCE.** Because most people travel back in time to take care of themselves as babies.

**SUE.** Really?

**BRUCE.** What better caretaker?

**SUE.** I guess so. Did you do that too?

**BRUCE.** I did. It's hard work.

**SUE.** I'll bet.

**BRUCE.** I was a big crier from day one.

**SUE.** You turned out okay.

**BRUCE.** Thanks.

**SUE.** Not too bad.

> (*pause*)

I certainly admire anyone who has the balls to raise a child.

**BRUCE.** Me too.

**SUE.** And I'll tell you what would keep me from doing it.

**BRUCE.** What?

**SUE.** The simple fact that they could die before you.

**BRUCE.** Oh.

**SUE.** And therefore what is the fucking point? Because that is a storm I could not weather.

**BRUCE.** Wow.

**SUE.** I guess it doesn't happen a lot but it does happen. I work in hospitals, I can tell you. And you think it won't happen to you, but I can tell you this with one hundred percent certainty – everyone thinks that until it happens to them. Doesn't matter. No one is safe. I know. I've seen it.

**BRUCE.** I agree.

**SUE.** You do?

**BRUCE.** I do.

**SUE.** I thought you were my counterpoint on these issues.

**BRUCE.** You're right. No one is safe. No one.

**SUE.** That's right.

**BRUCE.** When I went to the movies with my wife years ago I certainly didn't think I would be the only one eventually coming home.

**SUE.** You're married.

**BRUCE.** I was.

**SUE.** Oh. What happened?

**BRUCE.** An accident. You know, you talk of our base natures and machetes and all that, but when it comes down to it most people are just getting hit by cars. Nearly 50,000 people last year died in auto accidents just here in this country.

**SUE.** I'm sorry.

**BRUCE.** Thanks.

**SUE.** When was this?

**BRUCE.** Years ago.

**SUE.** You never mentioned it.

**BRUCE.** There never seems to be the perfect moment for such a conversational tidbit.

**SUE.** And you thought, why not the abortion clinic?

**BRUCE.** Exactly. What else to do in the abortion clinic? When there's no Rolling Stone.

**SUE.** I'm sorry.

**BRUCE.** That's when I was told that having children would be an impossibility.

**SUE.** Oh, wow.

**BRUCE.** To which, I thought, well, as I have no wife to speak of, I don't think that's a big problem.

**SUE.** Right.

**BRUCE.** So I get you. No one is safe.

**SUE.** No.

**BRUCE.** And yet we have our lives to lead, don't we?

**SUE.** I guess so.

*(A pause. They are both alone in their thoughts for a long moment.)*

**BRUCE.** It's kind of cowardly, really, when you think about it.

**SUE.** What is?

**BRUCE.** You know, cowering in the corner because of what might happen.

**SUE.** And what will happen.

**BRUCE.** Yeah, and what will happen.

**SUE.** If you're trying to get me riled up, it's not working. Because I'll agree with you on that point. I believe it is very definitely cowardly.

**BRUCE.** And that's okay by you?

SUE. It'll have to be.

BRUCE. It's not that I'm so brazen.

SUE. No?

BRUCE. No. Not brazen at all for a while. After the accident. No.

SUE. Of course not.

BRUCE. What does one do with that sort of information, you know?

SUE. A godless wilderness.

BRUCE. Well. Perhaps, yes.

SUE. It's hard not to come to that conclusion.

BRUCE. If God can't wake a sleeping truck driver, then what fucking good is he really?

SUE. Yeah.

BRUCE. Just a little tap on the shoulder. "Hey you, wake up…"

(pause)

But, you know, what are you gonna do? Not drive?

SUE. I try not to.

BRUCE. You still have to drive. And driving, despite it all, is a goddamn fun thing to do.

SUE. I don't know.

BRUCE. It is. It is. My trip out here. Was amazing.

SUE. I guess so.

BRUCE. I get it, Sue. I get it. Not much is safe. I get that. I definitely learned that little tidbit.

SUE. I'm sorry that you did.

BRUCE. But I get you. It's a terrifying prospect, having a child, isn't it?

SUE. I think so.

BRUCE. My wife and I had been deliberating about it.

SUE. Really?

BRUCE. Yeah. And, uh, after the accident. I just knew I didn't want to have kids anymore.

SUE. Yeah.

(**BRUCE** *is lost in thought for a moment.*)

BRUCE. But I don't know. I really don't know. I'm just thinking about all this....What if I was just...wrong... about myself?

SUE. What do you mean?

BRUCE. And like I was saying, you have to live your life, you know?

SUE. That's what they say on the TV.

BRUCE. You have to drive a car to get where you want...

SUE. Trains are pretty safe.

BRUCE. It's so fuckin'...Here we are all alone at an abortion clinic in Phoenix, Arizona. Think about this.

SUE. Think about what?

BRUCE. What brought us together, you know?

SUE. We like the same bar?

BRUCE. No. I don't think so, no.

SUE. What else could it be?

BRUCE. Because I don't know. I mean, what are we doing here?

SUE. Abortion. Remember?

BRUCE. No. Bigger than that. What got us here?

SUE. The Taurus.

BRUCE. Do you see this?

SUE. See what?

BRUCE. What am I doing here? I came all the way here. I drove here. Here we are.

SUE. I didn't ask you to come.

BRUCE. You see this, right?

SUE. What are you talking about?

BRUCE. What I'm saying to you, Sue, is that perhaps what has happened...is something extraordinary.

SUE. Nothing has happened.

**BRUCE.** They tell me I can't have kids. Suddenly, what? I
don't want them? Of course I don't. Because I can't
have them. And then...

**SUE.** So what are you saying? You're saying now you do?
You want children now?

**BRUCE.** Uh, you know...

**SUE.** What?

**BRUCE.** Yeah.

**SUE.** Okay. That's your prerogative.

**BRUCE.** Do you see what I'm saying?

**SUE.** Your life, Bruce.

**BRUCE.** Maybe there are gifts, you know? Sometimes?
Maybe there are.

**SUE.** What are you talking about?

**BRUCE.** You.

*(He points to her belly.)*

Both of you.

**SUE.** Funny.

**BRUCE.** You know, if I suddenly did believe in miracles then
this is one.

**SUE.** All right, Bruce. I get the joke.

**BRUCE.** I'm not joking. Look at me. I'm not.

*(pause)*

**SUE.** You want what? That we...

**BRUCE.** I don't know.

**SUE.** What? What?

**BRUCE.** Okay. That we walk out of here...

**SUE.** Wait...that we walk out of here?

**BRUCE.** And we go get a cup of coffee, of decaf coffee, and
have a conversation.

**SUE.** A conversation?

**BRUCE.** Yes. A conversation. Yes. About this situation. About
us.

*(pause)*

**SUE.** Bruce.

**BRUCE.** What?

**SUE.** And I am serious about this.

**BRUCE.** Okay.

**SUE.** Get the fuck out of here.

**BRUCE.** No. Why?

**SUE.** Get the fuck out. I am done with you.

**BRUCE.** No. Listen, all I'm saying is we talk…

**SUE.** As I'm sure you noted, there is security here, and as I am sure you will intuit, they will be siding with me the minute I start screaming for you to get the fuck out.

**BRUCE.** Just come with me so we can talk about the future.

**SUE.** There is no future. No future.

**BRUCE.** But, okay, if you don't want to be involved, maybe, I don't know, maybe I could take this child and raise him or her.

**SUE.** You're insane.

**BRUCE.** And can we go have this discussion somewhere other than an abortion clinic?

**SUE.** No. We need to be in the abortion clinic in order to get the abortion. I don't believe Starbucks offers abortions.

**BRUCE.** Because we kind of have to have it now. And I think we've been given this chance – this exceptional thing has happened…

**SUE.** No discussion.

**BRUCE.** Please. I need you to hear me out. Just hear me out…

**SUE.** …No…

**BRUCE.** …Let's just put the appointment off perhaps, for a day or two, let's just do that, okay?

**SUE.** No.

**BRUCE.** And let's just go outside, right now…

**SUE.** Stop. Bruce.

**BRUCE.** What?

**SUE.** You and I are done. With this conversation. With each other. For good. How do I know this? Because unless you walk out right now I'm going to scream...

**BRUCE.** Please don't.

**SUE.** Out.

**BRUCE.** Please.

**SUE.** *(loud –)* Leave me alone.

**BRUCE.** *(quiet)* Please.

**SUE.** *(louder)* Leave me alone.

   *(pause)*

**BRUCE.** Sue.

**SUE.** *(cutting him off – loud –)* Get out!

   *(Lights out.)*

## Scene Six

*(**BRUCE**'s apartment. **SUE** is at the door, in her coat. Uncomfortable.)*

*(A long beat.)*

**SUE.** I came back for the cats.

**BRUCE.** Okay.

**SUE.** Yeah.

**BRUCE.** Okay.

*(pause)*

**SUE.** And...I wanted to stop by.

**BRUCE.** I just...never thought I would hear from you again. A restraining order, maybe.

**SUE.** Yeah, well. Here I am.

**BRUCE.** Here you are.

**SUE.** Hi there.

**BRUCE.** Hi.

*(She fishes around for something.)*

**SUE.** Let me get that restraining order.

*(beat –)*

I'm kidding.

**BRUCE.** I wouldn't blame you if you did.

*(a beat)*

Come in, I guess. Do you want to come in?

**SUE.** Okay. I guess for a minute. Do you have a minute?

**BRUCE.** Yeah.

**SUE.** Or is this a bad time?

**BRUCE.** No.

**SUE.** Okay. You're not busy?

**BRUCE.** I'm just...Nevermind.

**SUE.** What?

**BRUCE.** No. It sounds stupid.

**SUE.** What?

**BRUCE.** I'm making a casserole.

**SUE.** That's not stupid.

**BRUCE.** Who makes casseroles?

**SUE.** You.

**BRUCE.** Me. For one. Come in.

(*She walks into the apartment. A beat.*)

Do we...? Can I take your coat? Is it...?

**SUE.** No, that's okay. We can keep it brief.

**BRUCE.** Coffee, or...

**SUE.** No. Thanks. Look. Let me just get to it.

**BRUCE.** You do like to do that.

**SUE.** What happened a couple of weeks ago. That was fucked up of you.

**BRUCE.** I know.

**SUE.** It really was.

**BRUCE.** I know it was.

**SUE.** I didn't begin to expect that from you and I was taken aback and reacted the only way I felt I could. I wish it hadn't come to that, but it did. You are hard to deal with sometimes. You are hard to say no to. And I needed to say no to you.

**BRUCE.** I know you did.

**SUE.** Yeah. You don't just spring that on someone at an abortion clinic. You just don't do that, Bruce.

**BRUCE.** Look. Whatever you need to dish out, dish it out. You want contrition, I offer you contrition.

**SUE.** I'm not trying to punish you.

**BRUCE.** It's fine if you are.

**SUE.** And I know it was not an ordinary situation. We hadn't slept.

**BRUCE.** So what? It's no excuse.

**SUE.** I don't know.

(*beat*)

**BRUCE.** You know what? I left that place just angry. But, you know, I had a three day drive coming back here, so…

**SUE.** So…

**BRUCE.** So I had time to think. And get a little sleep, you know?

**SUE.** Yeah.

**BRUCE.** And truth is, I was a lunatic out there, you're right. We hadn't slept. If I had had that thought any earlier than when I did, there in the clinic, I would've told you.

**SUE.** Yeah.

**BRUCE.** But I didn't. I, uhh, I'm sitting there and all of the sudden I have this bright idea, you know…

**SUE.** Yeah.

**BRUCE.** Which was not so bright…

**SUE.** Yeah.

**BRUCE.** It's just funny, really…

**SUE.** What?

**BRUCE.** How you have a whole life of knowledge and experience behind you, and suddenly you're willing to just drop it all. It's crazy.

**SUE.** No, I know.

**BRUCE.** I'm that much of a sucker? There's what? Suddenly miraculous events? A guiding hand out there? A greater meaning? I mean, there are just mounds of evidence in my life to suggest otherwise and there I am suddenly a sucker…

**SUE.** Don't be so hard on yourself.

**BRUCE.** I need to be hard on myself. Keep myself in check. I do. You know, it's simple, really, there are no miracles.

**SUE.** I guess not.

**BRUCE.** You know, and really, I wouldn't want there to be.

**SUE.** Why not?

**BRUCE.** Because the implications are just too terrible.

(pause)

So you know, I am very glad you are here…

SUE. You are?

BRUCE. I am. These past couple of weeks – I've been think-
    ing about you…

SUE. Why?

BRUCE. Thinking I just wish I had the chance to tell you
    in person that I am very sorry for my behavior. But
    the dumbass that I am, you know, I still don't have a
    number for you, do you realize that?

SUE. I wasn't sure.

BRUCE. That's how ridiculous I am.

SUE. You're not ridiculous.

BRUCE. Saying that shit to you in the clinic. I'm standing
    there, saying let's talk about having a kid and I don't
    even have your phone number.

SUE. It's not important.

BRUCE. No. There are no miracles. Just the stupid shit that
    befalls us.

SUE. Yeah.

BRUCE. And so, I am so sorry.

SUE. It's okay. Me too. I'm sorry.

BRUCE. Let's just…can we just call this thing even…

SUE. Okay…

BRUCE. …and move on.

SUE. What do you mean?

BRUCE. Everything cancels out. We're even. Here we are,
    no better, no worse.

SUE. Okay.

BRUCE. Which is better than so many run-ins you have with
    people.

SUE. Yeah.

BRUCE. You see what I mean?

SUE. I guess.

BRUCE. And really, seriously, beyond apologizing to you I
    should thank you.

SUE. For what?

**BRUCE.** For actually being a grounding force for me.

**SUE.** Me being a grounding force for you?

**BRUCE.** That's right. I can be a victim of my own enthusiasm if I'm not careful.

**SUE.** I don't think that's necessarily a bad thing.

**BRUCE.** It can be. It absolutely can. For me. You know, if I don't keep my feet on the ground, I...I what?

**SUE.** You fall down?

**BRUCE.** Yeah. I fall down on my ass. Which hurts. And looks stupid to onlookers.

**SUE.** Yeah.

**BRUCE.** So thank you.

**SUE.** Okay.

**BRUCE.** So maybe not even even. I came out a little better in the end.

*(sticks his hand out –)*

Shall we shake on it for poetry's sake?

*(Pause. She shakes.)*

**SUE.** Okay.

*(a beat)*

**BRUCE.** Thanks for coming by.

**SUE.** Yeah. Okay.

*(But she doesn't go. A long pause. Nothing is said.)*

**BRUCE.** How did it go?

**SUE.** How did what go?

**BRUCE.** After I left the other day.

**SUE.** Oh.

**BRUCE.** Yeah. How did it go? Did it go okay?

**SUE.** Oh. Well. It didn't go.

**BRUCE.** Oh. What do you mean?

**SUE.** You had me very upset.

**BRUCE.** No, I know. I'm sorry again.

**SUE.** I know.

**BRUCE.** You didn't have the abortion?

**SUE.** That day.

> *(beat)*

> Not that day.

**BRUCE.** Oh. Yeah. Right.

> *(beat)*

**SUE.** Did you think otherwise?

**BRUCE.** When I saw you here, maybe for a moment, I thought…

**SUE.** Does that upset you?

**BRUCE.** That you had the abortion?

**SUE.** Yes?

**BRUCE.** It upsets me…

**SUE.** It does?

**BRUCE.** …in that I'm guessing it's a sucky thing to have to do.

**SUE.** Yeah. Well, it is.

**BRUCE.** But if what you mean is am I regretful, then no.

**SUE.** Yeah. Okay. Me too.

**BRUCE.** Yeah?

**SUE.** Yeah.

> *(pause)*

**BRUCE.** But it went okay?

**SUE.** It did, yeah.

**BRUCE.** Good.

**SUE.** Yeah.

> *(pause)*

**BRUCE.** Seemed like a good clinic.

**SUE.** Yeah.

**BRUCE.** Good security.

**SUE.** Yeah, well. Yeah.

**BRUCE.** Clean. It's a clean…All right, I'm just rambling.

**SUE.** Yeah.

**BRUCE.** Okay. I guess this is it, then.

**SUE.** Yeah?

**BRUCE.** Yeah. Nothing really tying us together anymore.

**SUE.** No?

**BRUCE.** I guess not.

*(A long pause. Again, nothing is said. And* **SUE** *is not leaving.)*

You're still here.

**SUE.** Yeah.

**BRUCE.** Do you need more contrition? I have more. I can bring it on if you want.

**SUE.** I don't want any more contrition.

**BRUCE.** Then what else?

*(She doesn't answer.)*

Am I missing something here?

**SUE.** You're content to just call it even, or whatever the hell you call it, and do your stupid handshake, which, incidentally I am so sick of, and go back to your casserole? Is that it?

**BRUCE.** Well. Sue. I guess.

**SUE.** You guess?

**BRUCE.** Are there other options?

**SUE.** I don't know. I guess not. Now that your feet are firmly concreted to the fucking earth…

**BRUCE.** You confuse me.

**SUE.** You think I confuse you? You should see what I do to myself.

**BRUCE.** What am I missing here? I was a stalker who got stupid. I am sorry. We shook and agreed to cut our losses. Right?

**SUE.** That's what this is, cutting our losses?

**BRUCE.** Don't you think we should? Since our third date involved an abortion clinic, screaming, and a scuffle with security?

**SUE.** I should've figured…

**BRUCE.** Sue.

**SUE.** Yeah?

**BRUCE.** We barely know each other.

**SUE.** So?

**BRUCE.** I don't even know your last name.

**SUE.** You don't know my last name?

**BRUCE.** No. I don't. I know you told it to me. But, no, I don't know it, okay?

**SUE.** That's just…fucking priceless.

**BRUCE.** Look. I don't know what's going on here. The last I saw of you, you were screaming at me. And here you are…

**SUE.** Here I am.

**BRUCE.** And so what it is you want?

**SUE.** To…to…I wanted to see you. To talk to you. You know, we met…

**BRUCE.** People meet all the time.

**SUE.** We've gone through all this craziness.

**BRUCE.** These things happen.

**SUE.** I know they do.

**BRUCE.** They just happen. All the time, in fact.

**SUE.** No, I know.

**BRUCE.** It's not extraordinary.

**SUE.** I know.

**BRUCE.** It never is. Anything that happens is not extraordinary.

**SUE.** I know. Just the, what do you call it, the stupid shit that befalls us.

**BRUCE.** Yeah…

**SUE.** But here it is. In our laps, nonetheless.

**BRUCE.** So what are you saying?

**SUE.** And maybe it's not extraordinary and it's certainly no miracle, but here we are, Bruce…

**BRUCE.** Yeah. Here we are. And…

**SUE.** I didn't come all the way here to get my cats…

   *(a long pause)*

**BRUCE.** You really think this might be a chance for us?

**SUE.** I don't know. Maybe. I don't know anymore. And why is it so hot in here?

**BRUCE.** I'm baking.

**SUE.** I know. Me too.

**BRUCE.** No, I'm actually baking. In the kitchen.

**SUE.** Right.

**BRUCE.** Should I…

**SUE.** What?

**BRUCE.** You must be getting warm in that coat.

**SUE.** So what are you saying?

**BRUCE.** I'm saying do you want me to take your coat?

**SUE.** No. No.

**BRUCE.** I know it's a little hot in here.

**SUE.** It's hot.

**BRUCE.** Do you want to take off your coat?

**SUE.** No.

**BRUCE.** Okay.

**SUE.** Do you want me to take off my coat?

**BRUCE.** If you're warm, yes.

**SUE.** I'm fine.

**BRUCE.** Or to stay for a little while. I can make coffee.

**SUE.** I like tea.

**BRUCE.** Okay. Me too.

**SUE.** You do?

**BRUCE.** Yeah.

**SUE.** Then why did we keep getting coffee?

**BRUCE.** I don't know.

**SUE.** It's stupid. I like tea.

**BRUCE.** Me too. I prefer it.

**SUE.** Me too. You ordered coffee.

**BRUCE.** Because we called it "meeting for coffee." So did you for that matter.

**SUE.** You were having coffee. So...

**BRUCE.** Do you want some tea?

**SUE.** No.

> (*beat*)

> Are you having some?

**BRUCE.** No. Yes. I am.

**SUE.** I'm okay.

**BRUCE.** I'm making some anyhow. What type of tea do you like?

> (*He starts off but she stops him.*)

**SUE.** Bruce. You know, it was tremendously misguided, but you were really laying it all on the line out there.

**BRUCE.** It turned into lunacy.

**SUE.** I guess it did. But at least it was something, you know. And it got me thinking. And for whatever reason, I went against everything that makes sense and I came up here to see you. And I'm here. And I like you, Bruce. In as much as I know you. Which, admittedly, is not a lot.

**BRUCE.** We like tea. Who knew?

**SUE.** Exactly. And if you don't want to sit around here and have one more conversation in the abstract about things that we just don't get, then I agree with you. I'm tired of that too.

**BRUCE.** Okay.

**SUE.** I'm getting sick of my own voice.

**BRUCE.** Me too.

> (*a beat –*)

> Sick of my own voice. Not yours. You actually have a very pretty voice.

**SUE.** But you've taken a couple of stands with me and maybe it's time for me to take one too. Which is this: Bruce. I'm taking off my coat.

*(She does.)*

**BRUCE.** Okay.

*(He takes her coat.)*

**SUE.** Thank you. I was dying.

**BRUCE.** Let me turn off the oven.

**SUE.** Wait. Bruce.

*(He turns back to her.)*

Do you like me? Because I like you. I like you.

**BRUCE.** I like you, Sue. I've liked you since the minute I met you.

*(a beat)*

Now what?

**SUE.** I don't know. What do we do?

**BRUCE.** I don't know.

*(a pause)*

**SUE.** We could bowl.

**BRUCE.** Bowl?

**SUE.** Bowling. Go bowling.

**BRUCE.** Oh.

**SUE.** Remember? "Call me when you're back in town and maybe we can go bowling?"

**BRUCE.** Yeah. I do.

**SUE.** I'm sorry. It's a stupid idea.

**BRUCE.** I'll go bowling with you.

**SUE.** You will?

**BRUCE.** I like bowling.

**SUE.** I remember.

**BRUCE.** Yeah.

**SUE.** We haven't even been on a date.

**BRUCE.** I know.

**SUE.** Not really. We can just go bowl a game or two, right?

**BRUCE.** Why not? Why the hell not?

**SUE.** Okay, then.

**BRUCE.** Okay. When?

**SUE.** I don't know. Now? Is now too soon?

**BRUCE.** Now?

**SUE.** Is that too soon? Tomorrow? The next day?

**BRUCE.** No. Now is good. Now is okay.

**SUE.** Okay, good. Good.

>   *(pause)*

>   Shall we just…

**BRUCE.** Yeah, no. We can just go.

**SUE.** Okay.

**BRUCE.** Let me, umm…I was going to say get my things, but one doesn't really need anything to bowl, do they?

**SUE.** Just ourselves.

**BRUCE.** Okay, then. Let me turn off my oven. And off to the bowling alley.

>   *(He steps out for a moment.)*

>   *(She pulls out a scrap of paper and a pen, and is writing something down as he returns.)*

>   Are we ready?

**SUE.** Before I forget.

>   *(She hands him the piece of paper.)*

>   My number.

**BRUCE.** Oh, thanks. Right.

>   *(Beat – he looks at it.)*

>   Holmes?

**SUE.** Sorry?

**BRUCE.** Your last name. It's Holmes.

**SUE.** Yeah. It is.

**BRUCE.** Sue Holmes.

**SUE.** And now I have to confess I don't know yours.

**BRUCE.** Really?

**SUE.** I don't know yours either, no.

**BRUCE.** After the shit you gave me.

**SUE.** Yeah.

**BRUCE.** It's James.

**SUE.** James.

**BRUCE.** Yeah.

**SUE.** Well, then.

**BRUCE.** Yeah.

**SUE.** Nice to meet you.

**BRUCE.** Nice to meet you too…

>   (**SUE** *sticks her hand out – they shake hands.*)
>   (*Lights out. The end.*)

## ABOUT THE PLAYWRIGHT

Scott Organ's play *Phoenix* had its world premiere at the 2010 Humana Festival and its New York premiere at The Barrow Group. As a playwright, Scott's work has been commissioned by The Atlantic Theater Company, developed by The New Group and The Barrow Group, and has been performed and work-shopped throughout the United States. His full length play *Fixed* premiered at the Hangar Theater in Ithaca, New York. His play *City* was produced at the Circle X Theater in Los Angeles where it won the LA Dramalogue Award for best new play. It was subsequently produced at the 1st New York International Fringe Festival, directed by Tony Award winner Michael Rupert, and at The Flea Theater in New York, directed by Kevin Moriarty.

His short plays *China* and *The Mulligan* were published in *New American Short Plays 2005*, edited by Craig Lucas and have been performed throughout the country. His one-act play *and everybody else* can be found in *Best American Short Plays 2002-2003*. His short play *Afraid. Yes. Of.* premiered Off-Broadway as a part of The Fear Project at The Barrow Group. Many other short plays have been performed at the Atlantic Theater Company's 453 New Works Series, which he helped create.

Scott's screenplay *Better Man* was a 2008 Scriptapalooza Screenwriting Competition Quarter Finalist. He is also the author of the screenplay *Ghostkeepers* and the original television pilots *The Powerball 7* and *The Pines*.

# OTHER TITLES AVAILABLE FROM SAMUEL FRENCH

## SIRENS

## Deborah Zoe Laufer

*Dramatic Comedy / 2m, 2f*

When Sam Abrams first fell in love with Rose he wrote her a song which has been covered by every recording artist and translated to every language. It is heard in every elevator and on every cell phone ringtone. And for twenty-five years, Sam has been looking for the creative spark that this first flush of love had inspired in him – to no avail. Sam and Rose are now celebrating their twenty-fifth wedding anniversary with a cruise in the Mediterranean. And while on this cruise, Sam hears the most sublime music ever heard, jumps overboard, and winds up with a Siren. And there on her island he must struggle with the terrors of middle age, the tortures of creative failure, and the desire to live in his past rather than face his uncertain future. And he must find a way to get home and win his wife back.

# OTHER TITLES AVAILABLE FROM SAMUEL FRENCH

## THE HAPPY ONES

### Julie Marie Myatt

*Dramatic Comedy / 3m, 1f*

Orange County, California, 1975. For Walter Wells, it's the happiest place on earth. He has a beautiful wife. Two great kids. A house with a pool. Contentment. Until fate strikes a devastating blow, leaving Walter with no reason to put the pieces of his life back together. He resists attempts to help, especially the unexpected — and unwanted — offer from a Vietnamese refugee named Bao Ngo, who bears his own sadness. Then, across a cultural divide, Walter and Bao find a game to share, a song, a meal and then a way back in this uplifting — and surprisingly funny — new play by a rising star in American theatre.

**WINNER! 2009 Ted Schmitt Award for the world premiere of an Outstanding New Play – Los Angeles Drama Critics Circle**

"Wry and affecting…Myatt's characters are so engaging that it's easy to push them toward comedy, which tends to reassure rather than surprise us."
– *Los Angeles Times*

"…Understated power of this gentle yet gripping dramedy…The most impressive element of Myatt's new work is the dexterous way she elicits emotional resonance by giving the human frailties of the characters a weight equal to their innate compassion and goodness. Subtly depicting the overwhelmingly difficult process of mourning and letting go, Myatt leavens the tragedy without blunting its significance."
– *Backstage*

# OTHER TITLES AVAILABLE FROM SAMUEL FRENCH

## APHRODISIAC

### Rob Handel

*Drama / 1m, 2f*

Congressman Dan Ferris is being questioned about the disappearance of intern Ilona Waxman. Sound awkward? Imagine if he was your dad...

"A genuine thrill ride. As dizzying as a Nabokov-written episode of *The West Wing.*"
– *The New York Sun*

"Handel intelligently weaves together the threads of the story, and the characters shift voices and perspectives with little or no advanced warning... This lends much of the dialogue a witty, unpredictable texture..."
– *talkinbroadway.com*

"A cynical black comedy that's bathed in a kind of playfulness."
–*Denver Post*